Counselling and Curing

Thomas Häberle is a Benedictine monk who has successfully practised and studied natural methods of healing
for over twenty-five years. *Counselling and Curing* is a
sequel to *Helping and Healing* (Sheldon Press).

Counselling and Curing

Thomas Häberle OSB

Translated by David Smith

SHELDON PRESS · LONDON

First published in Austria in 1985 by
Veritas-Verlag, Linz, as *Raten und Retten*

First published in Great Britain in 1987 by
Sheldon Press, SPCK, Marylebone Road, London NW1 4DU

British Library Cataloguing in Publication Data

Häberle, Thomas
  Counselling and Curing.
  1. Naturopathy
  I. Title   II. Raten und Retten. *English*
  615.5'35   RZ440
  ISBN 0 85969 537 9

Phototypeset by Input Typesetting Ltd, London
Printed and bound in Great Britain by
Anchor Brendon Ltd, Tiptree, Essex

Contents

Contents

Foreword

My first little book, *Helping and Healing*, was, contrary to all expectations, extremely well received. It has found its way into very many homes, where it has become a familiar friend and is frequently consulted.

This is very gratifying and we could, of course, let the matter rest there. But I have received so many queries, asking me what I meant by this or that, or to explain something or other in the book more precisely or in greater detail. Experience has shown, then, that there is a constant need for improvements and additions to what I have already written. That is quite easy to understand! After all, we never cease to learn and no one can ever claim to be infallible. How could I, moreover, close my mind to these perfectly justified requests?

I first thought seriously of preparing a new edition of *Helping and Healing*, but when I saw how extensive the improvements and especially the more precise descriptions and additions would be, I had to reconsider this idea. A complete rewriting of the first book was out of the question. Clearly what was called for was a second book!

Foreword

This second volume is now printed and published and I sincerely hope that it will be as well received as *Helping and Healing*. It is the result of twenty years of experience and in many respects it can be seen as a commentary on the first. I have tried in writing it to satisfy the wishes of those readers and patients who asked me questions about *Helping and Healing*.

There is only one thing I would like to stress and it is this. The reader will not find in the pages that follow a systematically arranged series of prescriptions! He or she should rather read my descriptions, think carefully about them and make them fully his or her own. The final step is to find out what is right for him or herself.

Fr Thomas Häberle OSB

1

Memories

I have from time to time been told by readers and patients how much they would like to hear more about my youth and especially about the effect that my early years with my mother had on my later life and work. This is a request that I cannot ignore. I will satisfy my readers as well as I can in grateful memory of my dear mother, who passed into eternity many years ago.

I can see her now standing before me, a big, strikingly handsome woman with black hair and large, dark eyes. And I remember her above all when one of us had a pain, with a brown glazed bowl and a wooden spatula in her hands and a linen cloth over her arm. The bowl contained loam mixed with water and vinegar and she would spread this spongey mixture on to the cloth and press the cloth over the affected part.

A headache treated in this way would make me cry out in pain the next morning, when my mother removed the hardened loam mixure from my hair! I still use this treatment, but now I tell the patient to cover his or her head with gauze before the loam mixture is applied, so that it can be removed easily and painlessly. This loam mixture, which may contain other soil ingredients, often works better than the cabbage leaf treatment I described in *Helping and Healing*. I have found that patients who have not been helped by the cabbage leaf often respond very well to this treatment.

My mother once told me about a man who had been terribly burnt over more than a third of his body. Everyone was convinced he would die. A deep hole was dug in his garden, not to bury his body when he had died from his burns, but to contain his burnt body while he was still alive. The hole was filled up to his neck with good loamy soil and it was not long before his skin had grown again and he emerged from the ground completely healed. My mother always used damp soil whenever one of us had been stung by a wasp or a bee and it invariably worked very quickly.

Then there was the thirteen year old lad who had been suffering for months from severe rheumatic pains. He was told to drink two cups of elder-flower tea. For two hours he was quite delirious and then he had to pass water, which clotted into a white mass. But the boy was cured!

One memory will never leave me and there is a very good reason for that. There was at one time in our parish a young and energetic assistant priest living with the parish priest and helping him in his work. He was a gifted theologian and the nephew of a vicar-general. He was a friendly and very kind man, but he avoided company and was always deadly serious. There was something wrong! Mother was sure that it was his stomach that was troubling him and urged everyone she met to treat him with consideration.

This priest made a deep impression on me and,

although I did not know why at the time because I was no more than eleven years old, I felt strongly drawn to him. One morning – it was Low Sunday – I was serving at early Mass, because later that morning I had to deliver cakes and confectionery. It was this father who was saying Mass and I remember kneeling to receive the Blessed Sacrament from his hands. Sunlight filled the choir and the altar was bathed in light. The young priest was wearing his white Easter chasuble and distributing holy communion so worthily that I suddenly realized how beautiful it must be to carry out the priestly office!

One evening a few days later, I was watching my mother rearranging sweets and confectionery in the window of our shop and spoke about this to her. She turned round to look at me and asked me at once what I wanted to be. I told her I wanted to be a priest.

'Think no more about it, my boy,' she said at once. 'If you want to be a priest, you will have to be a much better person than you are now.'

I was convinced that she was right, so I thought no more about it at the time.

Six months later we heard the news that the assistant priest had died after a stomach operation. It was the custom then for the school children to be taken to the presbytery where the body was laid out and to say the rosary around the bier. He looked very peaceful. He was dressed in purple vestments and, to my surprise, his eyes were open.

When I got home, my mother told me: 'They should not have operated on him. If they had put linseed-meal poultices on him the ulcers would have broken open and his life would have been saved.'

'They should not have operated.' That sentence has remained with me ever since!

Let us now return to more everyday matters.

2

General Matters

It is quite likely that members of the medical profession may look at my two little books. They may read them out of pure curiosity. On the other hand, they may really be in search of useful information. For this reason, I shall begin by saying something about the complex causes of human illness and the way in which they are interwoven with each other.

It has often happened that one of my suggestions has proved helpful when doctors have failed to achieve a cure. In such cases, it does not really matter who has helped. All that matters is that help was there. That is surely the aim of all medicine – that sick people are restored to health.

Professional medicine can do a great deal, but not everything. If a remedy that is not officially recognized by the medical profession works, why should doctors refuse to accept it? Surely they should be modest enough to say: 'That remedy was successful. Why should I not use it myself? It will not harm my reputation. On the contrary, it will increase my patients' trust in me.'

As for myself, I certainly do not want to keep the

knowledge I have gained over the years to myself. I am very anxious to share it with others, so that they too may be able to help their suffering fellow-men. That is something that I see as serving the truth and as being answerable to God.

The Overspecialization of Modern Medicine

Most cases of illness are extremely complex. It is hardly ever possible to say: 'This organ is diseased. What must we do to make it function properly again?' We almost always have to say: 'Where is the source of this illness?' But we can only trace that source if we use the wholeness method to investigate which organ is causing the illness.

And this is a very sore point in modern medicine. Only recently I found some information in one of the Swiss daily newspapers which could without much alteration be applied to the situation in medicine in the whole of present-day Europe and North America. The medical correspondent told the readers of the paper that only fifteen per cent of the total number of doctors needed in the country were required to be specialists. At least eighty-five per cent of Swiss doctors ought to be in general practice. In fact, however, more than sixty per cent of doctors were specialists and only forty per cent were general practitioners!

What is the result of this overspecialization? In many cases, there is no longer any investigation into the real cause or causes of an illness. What often happens is that the diseased organ is simply treated with some medical preparation or by surgery. There may consequently be a temporary improvement, but the illness is not attacked at its source, with the result that the patient continues to suffer.

I am reminded here of a comment made by the nine-teenth-century philosopher Julius Langbehn who, because of his book *Rembrandt as an Educator*, became known as the German Rembrandt: 'God is a universalist, but the devil is a specialist.' I do not want to disparage real specialists, but what often astonishes me is how they cope with apparently incurable diseases. And I am bound to regard the complaint made by so many patients today as perfectly justified and criticize the way they as sick people are sent from one specialist to another, only to be told at the end of their long journey that nothing can be done for them.

The Complex Nature of Illnesses – Some Concrete Examples

I want now to give a few examples of illnesses and point to the way in which patients suffering from them can be completely and permanently cured. I will choose examples that are as typical and as representative as possible.

But let me begin by setting out the two rules that I always follow as a result of my experience of healing. The value of these rules has, I should stress, been confirmed again and again by my own observations and the evidence of my success in treatment. Firstly, I always make a whole diagnosis of the sick person. Secondly, I draw conclusions resulting from that diagnosis covering the whole person.

There is something else that I must stress at this point. Those who have read my first book will remember that I use the pendulum for diagnosis. This has to be done in a 'pure' manner. By this I mean that it is a serious misuse of the pendulum just to let it swing quickly over the supposedly diseased organ. How then, should it be employed? It is worth repeating here what I have said in *Helping and Healing* and perhaps adding a little to it.

The pendulum must be adjusted to the person who is to be examined. It must be orientated towards him as an individual. Then I am always very careful to swing the pendulum over the whole person, following the plan described in my first book. If this is not done, the diagnosis may be seriously wrong. In the same way, the person using the pendulum must work calmly and peacefully. For this reason, it is quite wrong to work beside the telephone. The person who is being diagnosed should not speak or ask questions or interrupt in any other way.

My first example is a twenty-eight year old man, Severin, who could no longer feel his hands and feet. There is a name for this illness, but it is so rare that I will not trouble the reader with it. What is more important is that the paralysis threatened to spread over the whole of Severin's body. He had chronic backache and walking was painful.

He showed me the results of previous medical examinations and I decided not to rely exclusively on these, but to carry out a pendulum test independently. I discovered not only the presence of toxic elements, but also that Severin had too much uric acid, too many white corpuscles, excessive coagulation of the blood and a serious vitamin deficiency. I traced the source of the poison to a benign tumour on the left side of his thorax. This tumour had formed within a fistula, in which there was a cyst. This cyst had originally caused the infection, which had raised Severin's blood sugar, although this high sugar level was not directly related to the pancreas. A similar condition was developing on the right side of Severin's chest, but there was as yet no sign of poisoning.

It was not difficult to see why his hands had lost their feeling. He had gout. This had also spread to both his shoulder joints. But why did he also have such terrible lumbago?

I continued with the diagnosis and found that kidney stones were preventing his kidneys from functioning properly. These stones may have formed because of the presence of fistulae and cysts on both the right- and the left-hand side of the pelvis. I also discovered that two of his intervertebral discs in his lower back had degenerated. This was because he had flat feet and had not yet been given foot-supports. There was also stiffness and muscular atrophy in his left leg, the result of a femoral hernia (see below, p. 27). Following the wholeness method that I have mentioned above, I knew that I was right to go to the source or sources of Severin's illness in order to heal him. I also recognized that an operation would achieve nothing positive.

I would like now to turn to a second, very complex case. Helga was about fifty. She had a fracture in her left foot, but no callous would form. Her doctor decided to try an operation to stiffen the tendon, but it was unsuccessful and Helga continued to find walking very painful. The doctor was insistent. If the fractured bone still did not grow together after three months, she was to have a second operation.

Helga came to see me. With the help of my pendulum and the wholeness method, I diagnosed a fistula with a cyst in the left-hand side of the pelvis. I told her to place cabbage leaves every night for three months on her left hip, reaching as far as the backbone, and to massage the site vigorously with olive oil every morning. It took three months from the commencement of this treatment for

9

the callous to form normally and the doctor was therefore able to cancel the second operation.

My wholeness method had proved its worth in Helga's case because the infection in the left side of her pelvis, which was probably the result of peritonitis, had been preventing healthy blood from flowing to the site of the fracture in her left foot and therefore preventing the normal formation of a callous.

I have described another case of successful whole diagnosis in *Helping and Healing*. The example that I gave there was of a man with apparently incurable bone decay who was given a year to live, but who is still hale and hearty ten years later.

3

Particular Illnesses

Depression

In this short section, I do not want to limit myself to mental depression as such. It is important to remember that many physical illnesses are directly related to this condition or are caused by it.

I would like to give as an example of this the case of Johann, an unmarried man of only twenty-four who was very deeply depressed. He behaved as though he was weighed down by a millstone on his breast. He was listless and unsmiling, saw everything in a very dark light and had a constant premonition of death. He was always close to tears and was unable to say why. The treatment that he was given as a mental patient brought no relief. Indeed, he got worse and worse. He began to have a deeply depressing effect on all those around him.

His tonsils had been removed and his teeth were suppurating. The dentist had looked at them and had declared them to be perfectly sound and healthy. 'I cannot bring myself to pull out such beautiful teeth,' he told Johann. 'Go and ask Father Thomas to examine you.'

11

When he came to see me, he was a picture of misery. It was not long before he was pouring out his heart to me. Then I took my pendulum and went over the whole of his body with it, examining each organ in turn.

I was very depressed myself at the end of my diagnosis, but I now knew the origin of his dental abcesses. Both shoulders and both sides of his thorax were infected and these together with his kidneys, his liver and the whole abdominal region were full of poisonous substances. It was very serious indeed, but I did not abandon the poor young man to his fate. I advised him to place cabbage leaves at night on the affected places and massage vigorously with olive oil in the morning. I also prescribed Haarlem drops and told him to drink Pastor Künzle's kidney and chest teas and to eat oatflakes — treatments I described in *Helping and Healing*. Finally, I suggested that he should massage olive oil into his jaw at least once a day. It took seven months, but Johann was restored to health and could go back to his work again. And he had not lost even one of his beautiful teeth.

Blood Pressure

Depressive people often suffer from low blood pressure. This is the result of internal infections. I treated one case which can certainly be regarded as a warning. Walter was in my class at the elementary school. I can still see him scratching on his slate during the handwriting lesson. He had a habit of blowing out his cheeks as he was writing!

Then I saw him again many years later, when he was about sixty. He asked me whether I could help him with his terrible depressions. I treated him for three months and he wrote to me, thanking me for curing him. But a year later I received another letter with black edges from his family. He had died of a heart attack on the railway station!

If only I had known then what I know now! Nowadays, I am not so easily deceived by an apparent result and am not simply satisfied with taking a patient's blood pressure at a given moment. If the pressure is relatively low, I always check the eighth and ninth thoracic vertebrae. In the case of very thickset people or when there is excessive calcification of the bones – this is common in old age – these vertebrae may be abnormally close together and even pressing against each other. This is a dangerous situation if left untreated and I now always try to loosen the compressed vertebrae by massaging the patient's back with olive oil and encouraging him to do stretching exercises daily or at least every other day.

Another serious case of high blood pressure that came my way was that of a fifty-five year old lady. The pills that her doctor had prescribed helped to lower her blood pressure a little, but she found they upset her in other ways. I tried olive oil, but this did not help very much either. Daily oatflakes also had very little effect. So I sent her to a chiropractor, who succeeded in reducing her blood pressure.

How is the following case of abnormally high blood pressure to be explained? Magdalene was seventy-two. When she got up in the morning and began her housework, her blood pressure was more or less normal, but as soon as she went to bed at night, it rose alarmingly. I came to the conclusion that she had vertebral compression. This was not harmful when she was standing or walking, but if she was lying on her side in bed, her vertebrae were pressed together, with the result that her blood pressure increased.

I have often been struck by the number of quite young and apparently healthy women who suddenly have a heart attack and whose lives are from that time onwards in danger. I have examined several women in that position and the cause has almost always been compressed vertebrae.

My conclusion is that it is certainly necessary to take the blood pressure, but that this is not always the decisive factor. The result may be deceptive and lead one to overlook the real cause of the illness. My school friend Walter is a tragic case of this!

Feverish Attacks

Erwin was an eleven year old schoolboy who had suffered for two years from repeated attacks of high temperature, sometimes reaching 38°C and occurring two or three times a week. It was so serious that he had eventually to give up going to school and his parents were obliged to pay a private tutor to give him lessons at home. Several doctors were consulted and they all maintained that these feverish attacks were caused by an infection, which they were unfortunately unable to identify. So I was asked to look at Erwin.

I found the cause of his illness on the left hand side of his chest, below his arm and towards his back. I told his mother to put cabbage leaves on the spot for two months and to massage it vigorously for two or three minutes every morning with olive oil. She also gave the boy two to three cups of Pastor Künzle's chest tea every day and a good helping of oatflakes.

The treatment worked, and his feverish attacks occurred less and less frequently. After two months he was completely cured and he was able to resume normal schooling.

Mira was sixty-nine. Her attacks of fever were so bad that she had to go to hospital. Like Erwin, she also had pains on her right hand side at the back, which made the doctors suspect poisoning of the liver, but they feared that it might be something worse. Could it, they wondered, be cancer of the liver? Should they take a section for examination?

My pendulum revealed an infection of the whole of the poor lady's right hand side, but the source of it was certainly not her liver. When her attacks of fever became less severe she was allowed to go home and I advised her to massage the infected side of her body regularly with olive oil. After two months of this treatment, Mira was able to go away on holiday and have a very enjoyable time, without any trace of illness.

The most difficult case of this kind that I have ever had was that of twelve year old Bernarda. She seemed to be always feverish. The doctors were puzzled. She was not suffering from tuberculosis, but what was the cause of her permanently high temperature of 38 to 39°C?

I found that her left shoulder was poisoned, close to her neck. I tried cabbage leaves and olive oil for three or four months, but this treatment only reduced her temperature to 37.5°C. I then experimented for months with various other treatments, but without success. I finally tried a pulpy mixture of aluminium acetate once a day before she went to bed and that soon reduced the girl's temperature to normal. Bernarda is now once again fit and well.

I must say a word in this context about cabbage leaves. You should certainly not go to the chemist's shop, but to your own garden, a farm shop or a good greengrocer. There are various kinds of cabbage, all of them good: white and red cabbage and one which Camille Droz especially recommends, Savoy cabbage. Only fresh large leaves should be used for healing – not the cabbage heads. And I would stress: only fresh leaves will be effective!

I have often been asked whether cabbage leaves from the deep-freeze are suitable. Of course they are! They may not be able to draw poison out of the body as powerfully as fresh cabbage, but they are quite effective and the great advantage of the deep-freeze is that they are available for healing throughout the year.

Uric Acid in the Blood

We all have uric acid in our blood – that is quite normal. But complications can arise if we have an excess of it. And many people suffer from that, often without knowing it. If you want to find out what it is, most popular medical books will give you the information you require. I will confine myself here to the illnesses to which it can lead.

Gout

Excessive uric acid in the blood can lead to gout, psoriasis, loss of hair and kidney stones. It can also cause a serious skin disease known as cellulitis, about which the French naturopath Messegué has had many valuable things to say.

What can be done about all these complaints originating with an excess of uric acid? I can reply to this question best by giving an example from the Alpine valley in which I grew up. I remember how the mountain stream close to my home used to swell after every storm and bring not only enormous quantities of water down into the valley, but also rocks, stones and branches and uprooted plants that had been growing on the banks. Almost every year it caused enormous damage and often flooded part of the valley.

The decision was taken to widen the bed of this stream and provide stronger embankments so that the torrent that followed the storm would be spread out and do less damage. But the result was disappointing. The embankments were torn down after the first storm and the water flowed over the banks again.

So it was decided to go to the source of the stream high up on the mountain and build a protective barrier there. The work took longer than the widening and the building of embankments lower down, but it put an end to the damage and the flooding.

What has this story of a Swiss mountain stream to do with gout? A woman's joints swell painfully and her hands and feet become a bad shape, and the joints become very stiff and difficult to move. The poor woman is in such pain that she cannot sleep. She goes to see the doctor. He gives her injections and prescribes tablets. He may even suggest that she 'takes the waters'. All this may help her a little, but she is not cured of gout. This is because, as in the case of the mountain torrent, attention is being given at the wrong place. Only the effects are being treated. The doctor is not going to the source of the trouble!

The most important thing I can say in this connection is this. An attack of gout in the hands and shoulders is always caused by an infection in the shoulders or the chest. Gout in the hips, knees and feet has its source in an infection in the abdomen.

To this I would add that kidney stones are almost always the result of infections in the lower part of the body. The cure should therefore begin there.

How does gout begin? The first sign is that the patient's hands and feet 'go to sleep', with 'pins and needles' in those parts of the body. The disease first attacks the tendons, then it goes on to the joints.

Where does it come from? It starts with an infection or a blockage in the lymphatic system. (I have written about this in my first book, *Helping and Healing.*) This leads to an excessive amount of uric acid in the body. People whose gall-bladders are too active are particularly susceptible to gout.

There is also little doubt that our present way of life favours gout. We spend too much time sitting. We use our cars rather than walk even a short distance. We shrink from the slightest physical exertion, and we eat too much fat and drink too much alcohol. It is not by chance that attacks of gout usually occur after large meals and evenings of heavy drinking!

But how does too much uric acid form in the blood? A person may, for example, suffer from severe influenza or pleurisy. Or it may be the peritoneum rather than the pleura that is inflamed. This results in cysts, fistulae and even non-malignant tumours forming. Such tumours are harmless, in that they are not cancerous. It may also lead to *ascites* (fluid in the abdominal cavity) or to *hydro-thorax* (water in the chest cavity).

Many heart complaints are caused by this and I need hardly say that, in such cases, it is not just the patient's heart that should be treated! The same applies to complaints of the bronchial tubes causing asthma – the patient should certainly not simply be given inhalations. No, we should go to the root of the trouble, draw off the water and attack what is pressing on the heart or making breathing so difficult.

But how often I find that antibiotics are automatically given in clinical treatment in order to overcome an infection caused by an excessive amount of white blood cells! The metabolic products of living bacteria, fungi and plants of a more developed kind are able to inhibit the growth of the infected microbes.

Doctors sometimes try to lower a patient's temperature with suppositories. His temperature may fall, but the poisons are not eliminated from his body. He continues to feel tired and listless and may take vitamin preparations. This treatment may be fairly successful in that the poor person gradually begins to feel less tired, but his body will still be full of uric acid and the effects of this will be particularly noticeable in his hands, feet, shoulders and hips. And this is all because the trouble is not attacked at its source!

The Consequences of Antibiotics and of Medical Ways of Reducing Body Temperature

This treatment of the symptoms without going back to the source can have very serious consequences. I have spoken above about gout and its effect on the joints. In addition to this, however, the skin can begin to itch or harden. Unpleasant rashes, eruptions and scaly areas can appear on the skin and perhaps the most dreaded skin disease of all, psoriasis, which is often regarded as incurable, may even develop. This is often accompanied by a loss of hair and kidney stones are often formed. These cause severe colic and unbearable pain. The patient sweats excessively, especially at night, becomes more and more listless and is increasingly prone to suffer from changes in the weather.

Whenever I reflect about cases that have been wrongly treated with suppositories or antibiotics to reduce the body temperature, I always think in particular of two very young children. Little Ruedl was only six years old. His hands and arms were badly swollen and all his joints hurt. He had such painful attacks that he could no longer go to school. He was always being given injections, suppositories and pills, but none of them was the slightest help. The doctors gave his illness an impressive sounding name, but I was sure it was simply due to a serious excess of uric acid in his body.

I had no doubt about the source of the infection or about the treatment. It would take a long time. I recommended laying on cabbage leaves and washing with camomile or bran – so that the skin would not become even more inflamed – and massaging with olive oil in order to get to grips with the source of the infection. I also suggested various herbal teas. These would, I believed, help Ruedl internally.

But how, I wondered, had the boy become so ill? When I questioned his parents, they told me he had been given strong drugs to combat rheumatism, regular doses of vitamins and powerful antibiotics. He had also been vaccinated and this had, I felt sure, sparked off his trouble.

Another very memorable but very unfortunate case of wrong therapy with cortisone and antibiotics is four year old Beat, who had been a perfectly healthy little boy until the end of the first year of his life. Then his tonsils became inflamed, he was always feverish and he set off on a long path of suffering. The cortisone treatment made his little hands swell up and nodes appeared on the joints of his fingers, which became very stiff. His little arms became very thin and covered with scales. The skin of his feet peeled and suppurated. The muscles of his legs shrank and both his knees became great unsightly knobs. The poor little boy could neither walk nor stand. It was not long before scales covered the whole of his body. He could not sleep and he made his skin worse by scratching. The doctors gave him a year at most to live.

But now, thank God, he is well on the way to recovery. I have every hope that he will, with time and patience, once again be able to live normally. The scales have already disappeared. His arms are again covered with light hair and he can hold a pencil in his hand. He has suffered so much and I hope to help him even more, but we must all be very patient! The healing ointments that I prescribed for the little boy's skin have been very effective, but I have still not penetrated to the root of this illness, so I do not expect them to bring about a permanent change. Gout, psoriasis and loss of hair all have to be cured internally. Otherwise, everything that we do will be in vain.

Phenomena Accompanying the Treatment of Gout
If one of my patients has gout, I ask him to use cabbage leaves at night and to massage with olive oil in the morning and also suggest that he has regular baths. But although he will expect the pain to decrease he may find that it increases, and that the joints affected by gout become even more swollen. So, in his disappointment,

he gives up the treatment. But that is the worst thing that he can possibly do. The fact is that the healing process has already begun. More blood is flowing in the direction of the affected parts and the olive oil beginning to have a deep effect. The crystals of uric acid are gradually being softened. This breaking down and softening process is, to begin with, very painful.

This is quite a normal reaction and it may continue for several weeks. The positive effects are felt only very gradually. The uric acid is slowly dispersed, the joints regain their mobility and the pain recedes. Anyone who wants to be healed of gout must be prepared for the phenomena that accompany the treatment. He must be patient and persist.

What internal treatment do I recommend for gout? As the deepest roots of the illness are to be found in the shoulders, chest and abdomen, it has always seemed to me that the lungs, the bronchial tubes, the peritoneum and the pleura should be purified. So I usually advise the patient to drink nettle tea without sugar in the morning, a cup of chest tea at midday and in the evening and during the day several teaspoons full of plaintain syrup or some similar natural product that disperses catarrh. I am not in favour of any products that contain Salyzin, because they may damage the hearing, nor do I recommend preparations which include codeine in cases of gout.

Kidney Stones

Angelika had terrible back-ache and after a while began to suffer chronically from colic. The doctor was not wrong when he said that she had kidney stones. But the urgent question was whether she should or should not have an operation.

I believe firmly that an operation should only be considered if there is no other cure. In such cases, I would certainly not advise anyone against an operation. I would never be so dangerously arrogant or so irresponsible in my attitude towards a patient. Who would want to have a sick person's death or permanent damage to his body on his conscience?

Angelika's case was, however, not so bad as that. I told her to place cabbage leaves on both of her hips, covering the backbone, at night and to arrange for an olive oil massage in the mornings. It was also important to rub olive oil every day for three minutes vigorously into the base of the spine.

There are two possible internal treatments not only for kidney stones, but also for gallstones. The first is to drink three large cups of warm, unsweetened nettle tea every day and to take a capsule of Haarlem oil in the evening before going to bed. Otherwise it is possible to take the equivalent of a small cup of holly tea mixed into the three large cups of nettle tea. The two kinds of tea must, however, be prepared separately, because nettle tea is infused, whereas holly has to be boiled. When each tea is ready, they can be mixed – six measures of nettle tea to one of holly tea. The mixture should, incidentally, never be drunk by the cup. It has to be taken warm and in sips throughout the day. This is because too much holly tea may have a temporary effect on the heart.

Each of these two internal treatments is to be preferred in certain cases. If I discover that cholesterol is present in the blood, I usually find that nettle tea and Haarlem drops produce good results. If, on the other hand, the patient is not suffering from an excess of cholesterol, but because he has stones of oxalate and bilirubin, then the mixture of nettle and holly tea is usually more successful.

Holly tea also has the effect of releasing and stimulating the flow of urine and for this and other reasons I find it the most reliable remedy in cases of gall and kidney stones. Its only disadvantage is that it is rather more troublesome to take. Whenever I am in doubt, I always let the pendulum decide.

Whether herbal or chemical medicaments are used in an attempt to heal a patient of kidney stones or any other illness for that matter, we should never forget that each person has to be treated as an individual in his own right. In other words, his treatment must be as far as possible subjective. In cases of sickness, it is quite wrong to treat everyone alike. Each person who comes to me for help or advice is for me a *tabula rasa*. I do not venture to suggest any treatment at all until I have examined him thoroughly.

I could easily write a whole chapter on allergies alone. How many people there are who cannot touch certain plants or fruits and how many simply cannot bear to have them in the same room! I just cannot say why this is, but there is no doubt in my mind that cerebral haemorrhage (see below) can play an important part in causing allergies.

Every human being, animal or plant is full of mysteries. We see only the external appearance of another person, an animal or a plant. Only God who has created them knows them through and through. Very few people have been given the grace to penetrate to the innermost being of another creature. Even fewer have the gift of knowing what another person is suffering from, simply by placing their hands, for example, on that person's body. I have to tell so many of those who come to me for help that I do not have that gift. I have to rely on what my pendulum reveals to me. People should not expect miracles from me!

In fact, I find it very painful when those who visit me regard me as a miracle-worker. I do not even possess any exceptional gift of healing! Any one of my patients must become aware of that after putting up with my cabbage leaf and olive oil treatment for two or three months. The healer is the patient himself or herself! That is very important to bear in mind.

But to return to Angelika. She persisted with my treatment, drank the mixture of nettle and holly tea and, when she went back to her doctor three months later for a check up, there was no sign of the kidney stones. Her urinary canals were no longer blocked and her legs were no longer swollen. She was cured!

I have found that, in many cases, swollen legs and feet are the result of blocked urinary canals. It is obvious, then, that it is not always an operation that is needed.

I remember one case in particular, that of a young man who had to have a very serious operation for kidney stones. He seemed to be well enough for six months afterwards, but, at the end of that time, he once again began to have painful attacks of colic. This time, however, he followed my treatment and the stones that had begun to form after the operation were dissolved of their own accord. A second operation would probably have been fatal or would at least have had a permanently bad effect on him.

Anyone taking nettle tea combined with holly tea

25

should keep strictly to the dose prescribed. Willy was seventy years old and suffering from gall and kidney stones. After two weeks of my treatment, he phoned me angrily, complaining of very painful colic. I endured his grumbling, because my pendulum showed quite clearly that there were no more gallstones in his body. Much later he admitted that he had drunk a blend of fifty per cent stinging nettle and fifty per cent holly by the cupful!

We are, after all, human beings and not powerful four-legged animals. They can obviously take much stronger doses than we can. There was a cow in the village which was refusing to eat and produced no more milk. The vet wanted to have her put down, but her owner was very reluctant because she was a prize animal. I prescribed a mixture of two litres of nettle tea and two litres of holly tea and within a very short time she was feeding and being milked again as before.

Human beings are quite different from animals and, on the basis of my own experience with both, I will have nothing to do with that naive but superficially plausible theory of evolution that claims that all living creatures develop of their own accord into higher forms of life. Perhaps, if those learned men who teach that theory spent six months working with cows on a farm, their theory would be radically changed by the knowledge they would gain. I know that, whenever evolution takes place and a living being reaches a higher stage of development, this process occurs by a fiat 'Let there be . . .' on God's part.

Man's recent flights to the moon have made us ask many questions, but they have done one good thing – they have shown the teachings of the great prophet of evolution to be absurd. He described in very poetic language how life would fly like an arrow from the womb of matter as soon as a certain age had been reached, that is, when matter had become sufficiently mature. But, if the moon and the earth are the same age, how is it that there is not a trace of life on the former?

Hernia and Prolapse of the Uterus

If inguinal hernia is diagnosed, but it is not strangulated and has been carefully manipulated during the initial treatment, it should not be difficult to correct without the operation that is almost automatically performed these days.

I always suggest that olive oil should be vigorously rubbed in for three minutes each day, working downwards and inwards from the loins into the groin, wiping the surplus oil off afterwards. The patient should be massaged in this way once a day for two months and, for safety's sake, it is a good practice to continue the treatment for a further period every other day.

If children or adults complain of pains in the lower part of their body, this may well be caused by hernia. After they have been healed, they should, of course, act sensibly and not overexert themselves.

Femoral hernia is even more painful than inguinal hernia. I am bound to mention it because it is such a common form of hernia, especially among women, who suffer from it more than men. It is usually caused by abrupt and violent lifting or pulling or by awkward physical exertion, when something suddenly snaps low down in the body, tearing the muscles and tendons. This is not necessarily accompanied by great pain to begin with, but it is not long before the patient becomes aware of the consequences. The abdomen becomes swollen, there is a constant need to pass water and, depending on the precise site of the rupture, the leg can become partially paralysed on the right- or the left-hand side down as far as the back of the knee. Crutches may have to be used – even by a young woman or a child.

A man in late middle age came to me once. He had a thin, narrow face and delicate fingers and was in no way inclined to fat, but his abdomen was very swollen and he suffered seriously from flatulence and was constantly passing urine that was as clear as spring water. He dragged his feet as wearily as a man who had just returned from unaccustomed mountain climbing. 'My doctor does not know what to do with me,' he complained. When I examined him, I found that he had bound his abdomen up very tightly and that there was great pressure on his respiratory organs. It was, of course, a case of femoral hernia.

On another occasion, a father came to me with his fifteen year old son Victor, who was complaining of pains in the abdomen and was beginning to limp. His doctor too had made a negative diagnosis. I used the pendulum very carefully and diagnosed femoral hernia on both sides of his body. I asked the boy whether he was an enthusiastic gymnast and sportsman and before he could reply, his father interrupted: 'There is going to be an end to your visits to the gymnasium! I have told you again and again! You are ruining yourself with your ambition always to be the first and the best!'

How should we deal with femoral hernia, then? If it is not too far advanced, the loins can be massaged downwards to the groin as in the case of an ordinary inguinal hernia, but continuing this massage down to the right and the left legs and along the back of the thighs to the hollow of both knees. This should be done for three minutes at least and the olive oil should then be dried off. The daily treatment should last for two to three months, after which the patient should be massaged every other day for as long as necessary. Great care should be taken during this later treatment to prevent another hernia occurring or the same one occurring again.

Prolapse of the uterus can be very unpleasant for women. I first encountered it when Jolanda came to tell me that she thought she had something wrong with her bladder or kidneys. 'I cannot hold my water,' she said. 'If I am in company, I dare not laugh aloud and sometimes I am even afraid to go out shopping. The slightest movement and I have trouble. My urine is as pale as water. Can you help me?'

What could she do to overcome this weakness in her abdominal muscles? The simplest and best treatment proved to be a daily massage with olive oil for two or three minutes from the vertebral column into the groin and then for two or three minutes from the loins to the groin as in the case of a femoral rupture. It took less than two months for her abdominal muscles to be restored to full strength and only a little longer for her problems to disappear altogether. She was a sensible patient during and after the treatment and that, of course, helped enormously.

I have often advised expectant mothers to massage downwards and backwards in the same way from the loins into the groin in order to ensure that they will have an easy delivery. This cannot harm the unborn baby in any way. All that it does is to make the tendons more elastic and enable the child to be born without complications.

I remember a long conversation that I had not long ago with a well-known gynaecologist about whether it was necessary to operate in the case of prolapse of the uterus. In my experience, massage with olive oil has proved successful in the great majority of cases, making an operation unnecessary. Most of my patients have also been able to continue with their normal household tasks during their simple massage treatment, so that their husbands and children have not been worried or overburdened.

So my conclusion is clear. Why should a woman have an operation if it is quite unnecessary? Surgeons too should be glad that my simple treatment is so effective, since it ought to relieve them of some of the burden of their work. There are also often after-effects and side-effects from surgical operations, but none at all from my olive oil massage. Sometimes, of course, to operate is the only possible course of action and in such cases I would never oppose an operation. But why opt for an operation immediately – as so often happens – without even considering an alternative first?

Bed-wetting and Diabetes

I do not want simply to repeat what I have already said in *Helping and Healing*, but I think it is valuable to draw attention to one or two important aspects of this problem. Like feverish attacks in both children and adults, bed-wetting must also be considered within the framework of a total diagnosis. Feverish attacks usually have their origin in cysts or fistulae in the shoulders, chest or abdominal region. The same applies when diabetes is diagnosed – it may have nothing to do with the pancreas. I prefer to avoid the word 'diabetes' in such cases and to speak of 'traumatic sugar' in the blood. As soon as the source of the infection is removed, this traumatic form of diabetes can be healed relatively easily.

In my experience, many children – and even adults – regularly wet the bed because they are suffering from traumatic blood sugar without knowing it. During sleep it is not possible to be fully aware of an excessive need to pass water and this leads to bed-wetting. The effects of this illness are really traumatic and the worst thing that a parent can do is to scold, mock or punish the child who does it – that can only cause him or her deep psychological suffering. In any case, punishment is also worse than useless. Bed-wetting is not due to perversity or ill-will. It is an illness.

The infection causing the excess of sugar in the blood has first to be traced to its source, then, and the next step is to treat the problem as every other infection in the shoulders, chest or abdomen is treated. The child should be given plenty of chest tea and as much oatflakes and rye bread as he wants. For the rest, however, he should follow as strict a diet as any diabetic until his blood sugar has become normal. Sugar can usually be replaced by honey without harmful effects, but chocolate, which is eaten in such quantities by children, should be avoided as much by those suffering from traumatic sugar as it should be by children or adults with liver or gall-bladder complaints.

Centre X

Disturbances in the level of sugar in the blood, then, can be caused not only by diabetes proper, which results from a failure of the pancreas, but also by what I call traumatic blood sugar, which has its origin in an infection somewhere in the body that has not been overcome.

But these are only two of the possible causes! Again and again in my many years of diagnosis with the pendulum, I have found that high urine or blood sugar can be traced back to neither of these. Its origin has been in a point situated in children 8 cm. and in adults 10 cm. to the right and left of the vertebral column at the height of the sacrum.

I call this point quite simply 'Centre X'. I have diagnosed disturbances in this Centre in almost every child who wakes up every half hour during the night. I have also found that massaging Centre X with olive oil soon puts this trouble right. And what about bed-wetting? If it is traceable to Centre X, it can also be overcome by massage.

It has become increasingly clear to me that, both in children and in adults, temporary disturbances in the blood sugar frequently originate in Centre X. The region has only to be massaged with olive oil. Even if this is not the site of the illness, the massage can do no harm at all.

These disturbances are not the only ones that begin in Centre X. My pendulum has pointed clearly to this Centre in cases of disturbed vision and even blindness, when specialists have been unable to find anything wrong with the eyes. A tangible improvement has resulted from rubbing olive oil into Centre X.

It is important to point out here, however, what universally applies in the case of disturbances resulting in bleeding in the head. The further back in the past the trouble lies, the more difficult a cure will be and, if the cells have been totally destroyed, there is no hope at all of a cure.

Complaints connected with an imbalance of chemical elements such as calcium and potassium in the body often originate in Centre X. Psoriasis has, in my experience, often been completely cleared up by massaging with olive oil in the region of Centre X. I have, however, never been able to discover whether all ugly areas of pigmentation have their origin in Centre X.

Progressive paralysis in the lower part of the back is certainly not always a sign of a spinal disease or, for example, multiple sclerosis. It may well be due to a disturbance in Centre X and therefore curable by rubbing olive oil into the lower part of the back. It is also helpful to massage the back of the thighs from the hollow of the knees upwards. The pain may increase during the first few weeks of this treatment, but be patient! Persevere and you will be healed.

If the trouble in the area of Centre X is due to an infection, then it is advisable to treat the patient with cabbage leaves as well as olive oil.

Centre X may also provide the key to the problem of overweight. An elderly farmer came all the way from South Tyrol to see me not long ago. He was really heavy and weighed 98 kg – almost fifteen and a half stone. I examined him with my pendulum and diagnosed a sugar problem. He followed my treatment – daily massage of Centre X with olive oil and a strict diet – and reduced his weight to 82 kg (just under thirteen stone) within three months. But even more important, his blood sugar was normal. He was breathing normally and his heart complaint had cleared up.

A fifty year old man had been suffering since childhood from asthma. He had received medical treatment for years and had often been to health resorts in the mountains, but all to no avail. I tested him and diagnosed a disturbance in his blood sugar located in Centre X. But his trouble was not high, but very low blood sugar! It took several months, but massage treatment of his Centre X raised his blood sugar and improved his breathing enormously.

Retarded growth in children is not at all uncommon and I have quite frequently traced the cause of this to a problem in Centre X. Most of the children I have seen have had either too much or too little glucose in their blood. Normal growth has almost always been resumed after massaging Centre X with olive oil.

I am bound at this point, however, to emphasize that all who diagnose a fault in the level of sugar in the blood with the pendulum should be careful not just to treat the patient for diabetes, but to ascertain first whether he or she has too much or too little blood sugar. Not to do this might have disastrous consequences.

What signs do I look for when I suspect that an abnormal level of sugar in a patient's blood has its origin in Centre X? Back-ache certainly, frequent passing of almost colourless urine, a dry mouth and constant thirst and sometimes disturbances in the vision. When these signs are present, I know exactly what to do.

I find it sad that many doctors refuse to recognize what I know from my own experience, reject my diagnosis, insist that the level of glucose in a patient's blood is not abnormal and sometimes even laugh at my reliance on the pendulum. But I am reassured by the number of cures that have resulted from my treatment of Centre X – they are sufficient confirmation of the correctness of my diagnosis!

Before leaving this question of treating Centre X, I

should add that I have often found it a very satisfactory way of dealing with troublesome epileptic attacks that are not localized in the head.

If only doctors and, even more importantly, medical students would take this question of Centre X more seriously! They would be able to carry out their task of healing more fully and help suffering people more effectively.

The Oil Test

So many people have said to me: 'What you have written is quite right, but who is going to tell me where to find the source of the infections?' Let me try to answer that question now.

In my first book, *Helping and Healing*, I described the 'oil test'. I apply it, for example, if a child wets his bed. I rub his shoulders, chest and abdomen vigorously with olive oil for two to three minutes, then I rub some fine cooking salt into the oil on his skin and finally dry it off. Red spots are still visible on his skin for several minutes after this oil test and these indicate the site of the infection.

They also indicate where the treatment must begin. I massage the child in those places with olive oil and treat him with cabbage leaves for two or three weeks at least, until he ceases to wet his bed, and then continue with this treatment for a further six to eight weeks afterwards to avoid a recurrence of bed-wetting.

This brings me to a second question, which I am asked even more frequently than the first: 'Where should I massage and for how long?'

The answer is simple: the oil test will show you where to rub and the length of the treatment is a matter of common sense! My main reason for writing my books has been to help people to heal themselves.

I must add a word of warning here, however. When a joint is worn out (as in osteoarthritis) or seriously deformed and has been replaced by an artificial joint, the region around that replacement joint should not be massaged with olive oil. It is possible that the oil will penetrate into the artificial joint, which may then become resinous. I cannot speak here of my own personal experience in such cases, but I am aware of the danger.

Olive oil cannot in any way harm natural joints, however. It does not attack the bones as marmot oil, for example, does. I always warn my patients to be careful in their use of this, as it can be dangerous and I have often found it in people's medicine chests. Canine fat may also be risky – I have no experience of it and cannot really say. But suspect fats and oils are best left alone.

Inability to control the bowels is even worse for a child than bed-wetting, but I have always found massaging with olive oil to be as effective in such cases as it is with women suffering from prolapse of the womb. Massage strengthens the muscles of the abdomen and intestines and the child will soon return to passing motions normally.

Migraine

I wrote a chapter in my first book on 'The Head' which I later regarded as upsetting, because, in my anxiety not to exceed a certain number of words, I had left many questions unanswered. I will try to remedy that state of affairs here and consider at greater depth some of the things that were discussed very briefly in *Helping and Healing*.

I read these words recently in a number of a medical journal devoted to nature healing: 'Migraine is still surrounded by mystery . . . Its causes have not yet been convincingly brought to light. It occurs five times more frequently in women than in men or children and for this reason its cause has been attributed to hormonal disturbances. But other causes have also been suggested, among them allergic reactions and structurally conditioned dispositions. There are also families with an exceptionally high frequency of migraine.'

Doctors, then, cannot throw much light on migraine. All that we can learn from medical books is that it is a form of headache attacking the sufferer from time to time either moderately or very violently. It is usually felt only on one side of the brain.

I think I have something to contribute from my years of experience to our understanding and treatment of migraine. I know that it can be caused in several ways. But what is more important, I have been able to eliminate it in so many cases that I feel I have to offer what help I can to those who suffer from it.

It is a very severe form of suffering. I have taught girls who were in such pain that they were often in tears during lessons. I have known women whose pain has been written visibly on their faces. I have met men who have been in despair because of the headaches that have tortured them by day and night.

Temporary relief can be gained from pain-killing tablets prescribed by the doctor, but after an hour or so the pain returns with renewed violence. I have often heard of doctors speaking, in such cases, of ulceration of the jaw, suppuration of the maxillary sinus, dental abscesses, inflammation of the trigeminal nerves, strangulated nerves, catarrh in the frontal sinus and middle ear, injuries within the head, meningitis and other disorders and even recommending an operation! And yet it was none of these things – merely migraine.

People suffering from migraine almost always complain of a number of other problems. They have, for example, a stiff neck and have great difficulty in turning their head. They have a bad memory. They cannot concentrate. There is a constant buzzing, humming noise in their head. They cannot see or hear properly. They lose their sense of taste or smell. They have attacks of dizziness. They want to vomit. They suffer from insomnia.

When I carry out a pendulum test with one of these poor people, I never confine it simply to his head or the defective organ that he has complained about. I examine all the organs I have just mentioned and take a sounding of the whole body, bearing in mind the complexity of the disorder. With the pendulum, I can always go to the source of the trouble! If the patient complains of migraine or recurrent headaches, I always try to find out whether this is caused by an organ in his chest or abdomen. A stomach disorder can, after all, cause headaches! Perhaps his gall bladder is causing the trouble. Or it may be diabetes. Is it perhaps his spinal cord? It may even be due to a hormonal disorder.

Many remarkable things may be brought to light by a pendulum test of the whole body and each of these has, of course, to be understood as clearly as possible. But my experience has taught me that, in the vast majority of cases of so-called migraine and even of more general headaches, the trouble begins in the head itself. It would be a pity if all the valuable knowledge that I have acquired were to be lost, so I shall in the next few pages discuss some of the cases of 'headache' that I have diagnosed and treated in the hope that some fundamental guidelines can be derived from them.

Cerebral Haemorrhage

During the winter months, Anton goes tree-felling, but this work has become almost impossible for him. He comes to me complaining of raging headaches. He has been taking pills and tablets, but they are making him even worse, he thinks. It is so bad that he can hardly bear to go on living.

My first question is: 'Have you had a fall while you were working or have you had a blow on your head?' and at once he bends his head forward and shows me a scar. 'A heavy branch fell on my head years ago when I was cutting trees in the forest,' he tells me. 'The pains in my head began then. And they have got much worse since.'

With my pendulum, I diagnose a blood-clot eight cubic centimetres in size in his skull, towards the back, low down and on the left-hand side. Using encephalography, the doctors who examined him after the accident discovered nothing!

I tell Anton to have his head massaged for three minutes every evening for a minimum of two months, making sure the olive oil penetrates into the roots of his hair and that his head is dried afterwards, and washing his hair no more than once a week and then in the morning. To protect his bedclothes from the oil on his head, he should put a cloth on his pillow. I had a letter from him two months later – at the end of his period of treatment: 'I have no more headaches!'

Olive oil has one really exceptional quality: it can penetrate into the hardest of bones. It penetrated Anton's skull and slowly but surely softened the coagulated blood inside until the clot was eventually removed.

It is similar in the case of gout. The pressure on the head may increase during the first few weeks of treatment, with the result that the pain is more intense. As the treatment proceeds, however, the pain becomes less, until the patient is finally set free from his suffering.

But do not be disheartened if your headaches return when they have disappeared completely after two or three months of the olive oil treatment! This is because surplus water has accumulated later in the cerebellum. The remedy is very simple. Put a cabbage leaf low down on the back of your head at night and massage the spot in the morning.

Without wanting to cause further discouragement, however, I have to add here that you may have headaches again even after using olive oil and cabbage leaves! My advice in that case is to treat the cerebellum, which is situated at the lower part of the head and the top of the neck, every six months for a few weeks with olive oil and cabbage leaves. These can never do any harm even if you have nothing at all wrong with you.

I say this quite emphatically because I do not want people to think that all those who use the pendulum are ignorant charlatans. Some of course are, and many of them have been publically criticized.

I have to admit that there have been patients who have not been made well by my treatment. Why, when they have followed my advice, only God knows. Some of them, of course, have not co-operated conscientiously. They have told me afterwards: 'I did what you told me for two or three weeks, but there was no improvement, so I stopped.' In such cases, the blame is not with the pendulum but with the patient, surely.

And all who use the pendulum should take great care not to confine themselves just to the back of the head and the neck, but to examine the whole forehead between the temples and the whole of the skull from ear to ear. This is the only way of telling precisely where the head has been struck in an accident – at the front, on the top of the skull or at the back. The bleeding is usually more copious within the skull at the point where the blow struck.

I have often come across really remarkable things when people who have had head injuries have come to me. A powerfully built young man told me not long ago that he had been suffering for months from terrible headaches. I let my pendulum swing over him and found that he had been bleeding inside his skull. I asked him whether he had recently received a blow to the skull and he at once replied: 'I was in a café one evening and got into a fight with another man who had been drinking too much. He picked up a beer bottle and hit me on the head with it.'

I decided on the following treatment, which proved to be very successful: the forehead was to be thoroughly massaged with olive oil for ten weeks, the whole of the skull from ear to ear for twelve weeks and the back of the head and the upper part of the neck for ten weeks. In addition to this he was to place a cabbage leaf in the evening on his neck after rubbing with olive oil and then drying it off for at least four weeks after beginning the cure. He was also to wash the back of his head and neck in the mornings during the cabbage leaf treatment.

It no longer surprises me that my patients often fail to

understand my diagnosis and my treatment. This almost always leads to failure! Let me give an example of this.

A very respectable and well-off lady wanted to know why she was tortured with migraine day and night and why the doctors she had consulted could do nothing about it. She had for the most part been given pills and told: 'Take them before you go to bed. They will kill the pain and at least you will be able to sleep at night.'

My pendulum showed that there had been bleeding in her head from the right hand side of the forehead over the skull to the back of the head. She went skiing every winter. Her headaches dated from the time that she had had a serious fall and had struck her head!

'You will have to massage the whole of your head once a day for three minutes with olive oil. The treatment will last for three months.'

'What do you mean? I have a senior position in my company and it would be impossible for me to go around with oily hair all day! Surely you have some other treatment – a herbal tea perhaps or some other medicine?'

I tried to pacify her: 'It will only be for three months at the most and you will be cured. I do not know of any teas or medicines that would be effective in your case.'

'Do you mean, then,' she asked, 'that you are going to leave me with this terrible headache and not help me?'

'My dear lady,' I replied, 'If you do not agree to the olive oil massage, there is only one alternative. You can have an operation. That means sawing through the top of your skull and removing the coagulated blood surgically.'

She was obviously very angry, because she got up without a word and left the room, slamming the door behind her.

A month or so later I received a phone call from her.

'I am sorry I was so brusque when I came to see you, Father. But is there really no other treatment apart from that terrible olive oil massage?'

'If there is,' I said, 'I do not know of it. But you could wear a wig for three months or you could treat your hair every morning with a dry shampoo.'

If only, I thought, the good lady had begun the treatment when she first came to see me! She would by now be well on the way to being cured!

For the most part, people come to me because they have been recommended by someone I have successfully treated. How often I am asked: 'You helped so-and-so. Can you help me too?'

Inner Voices, Somnambulism and Epilepsy

A well-known artist and teacher, who lived in a beautiful old manor-house, consulted me once because, as he put it, 'a priest is bound to know about occult matters'. He began at once to tell me about his home.

The house was now legally his property, but the previous owner was apparently still claiming that it was his. He was widely known in the district as an obstinate, querulous and cross-grained man and the new owner could make no headway with him.

But what was worse was that he heard voices during the night! It was in fact the voice of his dead wife, reassuring him: 'You are the legal owner of the house now. Stay here! No one can take it from you.'

He found it so uncanny that he could no longer sleep under his own roof. Would I as priest exorcise the house for him?

'I will bless it for you if you like,' I replied and did it within the next few days. At the same time, I took the

43

opportunity to examine it for subterranean watercourses and to screen it off against radiation, using radio-aesthesia. Then I went away and thought no more about it.

Twelve months later, I heard from the artist again. Nothing I had done had helped at all, he complained. He was at the end of his tether – a nervous wreck!

This time I carried out a diagnosis of the poor man himself with the pendulum and found that there was excessive pressure on his cerebellum. I prescribed the cabbage leaf treatment on the site for two months.

'Do not be surprised if there are drops of water on the leaf in the morning, where it has touched your skin,' I warned him. 'After you have removed the leaf, rub your neck vigorously with olive oil for three minutes.'

Another year passed before I saw him again. But when I did encounter him, he told me at once and with obvious happiness that he had not been disturbed at night for a long time and he was certainly no longer a nervous wreck. But what pleased him most was that his work as an artist had not suffered in any way.

'Quite the opposite, in fact,' he assured me. 'Now that I no longer hear inner voices, my artistic inspiration has increased.'

It may be mischievous of me, but I cannot help wondering: 'There are so many modern painters and sculptors who – if they took my advice and put a cabbage leaf on their neck at night and massaged with olive oil in the morning – might produce much more normal pictures and sculptures.'

And writers! Cross-grained and critical men writing in the secular and even in the religious press, some of them even authors of spiritual books! They may not be hearing inner voices and needing olive oil and cabbage leaf therapy, but kidney tea might cure the disorder of the gall-bladder from which they are obviously suffering. Even Nietzsche once said: 'They spew up their gall and call it a newspaper!'

But, at a more serious level, the problem of sleep-walking can cause deep anxiety. A father once told me: 'My nine year old daughter is a sleep-walker. She does it especially when there is a full moon. We are very worried.'

The man brought the little girl to me. There was no visible sign of any defect – she seemed physically and spiritually quite normal. But my examination of her with the pendulum revealed excessive pressure on the cerebellum. After a period of therapy with the cabbage leaf at night and two minutes' massage with olive oil in the morning, her sleep-walking ceased!

From what I have said so far it is possible to draw this conclusion: many disorders of the head and the nerves can be traced back to one of two basic facts. The cause of a disturbance in the head is either a haemorrhage within the skull that does not permanently injure the brain or excessive pressure on the cerebellum, sometimes connected with an inflamed pituitary gland. I have already indicated what should be done in each case. One of these two causes is quite often at the root of what has been diagnosed and treated as epilepsy. The correct treatment will result in a cure!

At this point, I am bound to emphasize that patients who have for years been receiving drugs from a psychiatrist should on no account give them up abruptly. They should break the habit very gradually if they want to avoid a dangerous shock reaction or a relapse, possibly causing serious damage that may be very difficult to rectify. What I always say in such cases is: 'It is better to take drugs for a further month than to cause a crisis.' After all, the psychiatrist himself will, as time passes, become aware of an essential improvement in his patient and reduce the drug dose accordingly.

It is surely sensible to examine those who claim they have been experiencing apparitions or visions for cerebral disturbances of the kind that I have just described. This applies particularly to visions of a religious nature. I would also include natural cases of hysteria and an almost unconscious desire to deceive themselves and others on the part of people who in good faith talk of their religious experiences. A word with or a note written to their confessor or spiritual director is often very useful in such cases.

Let me give one example. A man campaigning for the canonization of a servant of God wrote to me some time ago for advice. A very respected person had written him a letter, insisting that the servant of God had appeared to her several times during the night and had given her messages and had made revelations concerning the future. What, he asked, did I think of this claim?

I examined the lady's nervous system and diagnosed excessive pressure on the cerebellum coupled with a change in the pituitary gland. It was quite clear to me what the problem was and I gave the man the information he required.

I have nothing at all against authentic visions that are recognized by the Church. The great Saint Teresa of Avila was, for example, too sober-minded and self-critical to fall a victim to self-deception. And I would never venture to accuse the great prophets of the Old Testament of having morbid ideas. The Holy Spirit was speaking through them. But no one can have failed to notice how many very dubious pseudo-religious messages are being proclaimed in the world today! I am very reserved in my attitude towards them and prefer to cling to the Church's judgement of them. Throughout history, authentic teaching has always passed the Church's tests. And then there are the words of our Saviour himself: 'By their fruits you will know them' (Matt. 7.16,20).

It is true to say that, in our very materialistic and rationalistic age, the extremes seem to exist side by side. On the one hand there is a radical rejection of everything supernatural and, on the other a morbid preoccupation with the miraculous. Both are wrong. The truth is somewhere in the middle.

Do not misunderstand me! I believe in the appearances of our Lady at Lourdes and Fatima which have been validated by the Church. But I believe even more strongly in the doctrinal pronouncements of the Church about the Immaculate Conception of Mary and her Assumption, body and soul, into heaven. There would not be so much dangerous enthusiasm and sectarianism in the Church if this were taken to heart! What the world regards as 'religious' is by no means always authentic religiosity.

Disturbances in the Senses

I have already said that people often come to me complaining of constant headaches. Sometimes I encounter people whose aching head is accompanied by diminished vision or hearing. Others complain of a loss of the sense of smell or taste. Some tell me they have a permanently salty taste in their mouth.

Barbara was about forty. I had known her since childhood. 'What can I do?' she asked me. 'I have a raging headache all the time and my mouth feels as though it is full of salt. Should I go to the dentist?'

My pendulum showed that she had had a haemorrhage in the central part of her skull near the ethmoid bone. I advised her to rub olive oil every day into her forehead, the top and back of her skull and her upper neck and to keep up this treatment for several weeks.

One day, after the massage, she became aware of a little plug of blood in her mouth and her saliva was strongly flecked with blood. From that time onwards, her headache disappeared together with the bitter taste that she had had for so long.

I have always found that, as soon as the coagulated blood in the skull has been dispersed, the patient's vision and hearing return to normal and he gradually recovers his sense of smell and taste. In my experience, glaucoma is often caused by a cerebral haemorrhage or excessive pressure on the cerebellum.

Let me illustrate this by a case I treated not long ago. Bernhard was a thirteen year old schoolboy whose sight was becoming worse and worse. Stronger glasses brought no improvement. His doctor sent him to the eye clinic, where he was at once told that he had glaucoma. There was no hope of a cure at his age.

When his parents brought him to me, I told them to massage the back of his head and his neck each evening for three minutes, making sure the skin covering his skull was really soaked in olive oil, then to dry the surface thoroughly. One morning each week they were to wash the back of his head with warm water. Once a day he was also to bathe his eyes in salt water.

His sight was gradually restored and, only three

months after beginning this treatment, the eye specialist was able to say that Bernhard was no longer suffering from glaucoma. He came to me for aftercare and, after confirming that he could now see perfectly, I recommended that the massage should continue for a few weeks so that the last traces of clotted blood should be dispersed at the back of the boy's head. He also continued, on my advice, to bathe his eyes once a day.

Pia is another very interesting case. This little girl of four was, according to the doctor's diagnosis, suffering from an incurable condition – hydrocephalus or water on the brain. Although a little tube had been inserted into her head by surgical operation to drain off the fluid, her father and mother were still unhappy and brought her to me.

I saw at once that both parents had very powerfully developed skulls. It was only to be expected, then, that their daughter's head should be equally large and powerful. Then I discovered, with the aid of my pendulum, that she was suffering not from water on the brain, but from pressure on the cerebellum.

Pia's parents placed a cabbage leaf each night and rubbed in olive oil for two minutes every morning not only on the upper part of her neck, but also on her shoulders at the point where they joined her neck. The cabbage leaf extracted a great deal of water and now Pia looks like a normal child and is beginning to eat, sleep and speak normally.

I very well remember how my father, God rest his soul, sometimes took my hand when I was a boy and drew it over his head. I could feel a long depression in his scalp. His teacher, he told me, had been furiously angry one day and had struck him on the head with his rod. Later, the man had been removed from his post and had become a prison governor.

So much for human kindness in our schools! But how wrong it is for those in charge of children to give way to uncontrollable anger and behave violently. A nun once told me that she was permanently tormented by headaches and, when I examined her, I found a haemorrhage at the back of her head. One of the teachers at her school had a very quick temper and once, when she could not answer a question promptly, this teacher had seized her by the hair and dragged her to the floor. She had not dared to tell anyone at home about it at the time, but she had suffered from headaches from then onwards.

My pendulum has often brought very painful things to light. An apparently happily married woman came to me once, complaining of headaches and dizziness. 'You have a flow of blood from the forehead to the back of your skull,' I told her. 'You must have been struck violently on the forehead.'

She began to cry. 'My husband was furious one day and hit me with his fist on the forehead. He knocked me unconscious . . .'

Many people who come to me complaining of migraine tell me their fathers or mothers were often angry and violent and hit them on the head for trivial offences.

Hay Fever and Running Nose
I have already written in my first book about what to do if you suffer from hay fever. Bathing the face will undoubtedly bring considerable relief, but it will not, of course, go to the root of the problem.

My experience over the years with the pendulum has proved to me beyond all doubt that hay fever and rhinitis leading to a running nose have their origin, like so many other head complaints, in cerebral haemorrhage. As in the case of migraine, then, the clotted blood has to be removed from the skull by massaging over a fairly long period with olive oil. 'A fairly long time' may mean ten months of massaging before the nose ceases to run.

Having begun to speak of the effects of a flow of blood in the head, it would be foolish not to mention some of the strikingly successful cures that have come my way recently.

It is a well established fact that cerebral haemorrhages exist, but what is not known is that they are much more common than is usually believed. A young woman studying anatomy in Germany, who was able to free herself completely from the migraine that was torturing her by massaging her head with olive oil, told me this. Later, at my request, she confirmed what she had said to me in a written statement: 'The department in which I am studying specializes in the dissection of human brains. On average, out of every ten heads that are dissected in our laboratory, six have had cerebral haemorrhages. Plugs of blood as big as chickens' eggs have been found in these dissected brains. What is really remarkable is that they were not brought to light by X-rays.' (This confirms my own experience in the case of gall-bladder X-rays.)

How many suffering people could be helped in apparently hopeless cases if only we had faith in the power of olive oil! I think this is certainly borne out in the examples that follow.

Elizabeth was a young married woman, the mother of twins. One winter, she slipped on ice in the street and struck the back of her head on the pavement. She was taken home unconscious. When she eventually came round, she felt dizzy and her vertigo continued. Indeed, it became so bad that she dared not go out of the house. Her doctor did not know what to do about it and sent her to the university clinic. The doctors there advised her to have an operation. I advised her against it. After three months of my olive oil treatment, her headaches and giddiness had gone for ever.

Johanna is thirty and a domestic servant. When she was only nineteen she had a bicycle accident, hitting her head on the road and causing blood to run out of her nose and ears. She did not tell her employer. As time went by, she became conscious that she could not see or hear so well and went to the eye clinic at the hospital. The specialist examined her eyes and told her: 'There is nothing I can do. You are going blind.'

Despairing, she came to me. I recommended the olive oil and cabbage leaf therapy on the upper part of her neck and salt water eye baths. She had also had very irregular periods and leukorrhoea since her accident. Pastor Künzle's tea for women soon put that right. Johanna has not gone blind. I am pleased to say she has no more physical troubles since receiving the right treatment.

Stefan is only eleven and a keen gymnast. He fell from the horizontal bar onto his head. It was not long before his hearing began to fail. The ear specialist could find no cure and so his mother brought him to me. My pendulum helped me to diagnose an internal haemorrhage blocking the auditory nerve. After only three weeks of olive oil massages, Stefan's mother wrote to me with the good news that her son had run to her the other day in high spirits: 'Mum, there was a kind of explosion in my right ear and now I can hear again!'

Sometimes, but not always, underground watercourses and radiation from the earth can be blamed for retarded growth or mental development in children, but this can also certainly be caused by internal bleeding in the head. I think this can best be illustrated by the case of Josef, a young pupil in a convent school that I often visited.

The headmistress asked me one day: 'What can I do about Josef? He is a real nuisance – you never know what he is going to say or do. He is not stupid, but his school work is terrible.'

With my pendulum I diagnosed a cerebral haemorrhage brought about by a fall in the school playground and the presence of stones in his gallbladder and prescribed the olive oil treatment. Three months later, I received a phone call from the sister: 'Josef is the best pupil in his class now and gets on well with everyone.'

I could also give examples of children whose speech and even movement were inhibited by a haemorrhage in the head, but who can now speak and walk. Since the relevant nerve centres have been unblocked by the dispersal of the coagulated blood, they have been able to develop normally.

And what about children suffering from cerebral paralysis? This is, in my opinion, an area in which there should be a large number of successful cures. But again and again we hear the words: 'We are too busy to deal with such cases in our general practice . . . our clinic . . . our hospital . . .'

Barbara was only eighteen months old. She had severe convulsions and had to be kept in bed. Drugs brought only temporary relief. Her father travelled a long way to see me. He was in great distress. I diagnosed a haemorrhage that had been caused by a blow to the head in early infancy and prescribed olive oil massages. Only two days later, I received a phone call: 'Barbara had a nosebleed this morning . . .'

Ernst was fourteen and still at secondary school. He was suffering from depression, vertigo and severe headaches. He was so ill in fact that he had not been to school for months. His doctor was treating him with drugs for a psychological disorder, but without success.

His despairing parents asked me to examine him and I at once found he had gallstones and high blood sugar. This was a relatively unimportant problem. (I have already said how it can be dealt with.) More serious was the haemorrhage I discovered in his head, caused by a fall – the boy was a keen gymnast and cyclist.

His parents did exactly what I told them to do. They did not cease giving him the drugs that the doctor had prescribed – that decision had to be left to the doctor himself. Almost a year went by and I received a couple of phone calls from Ernst's mother, the second to say he had been completely cured.

The most serious case was, however, that of Edgar, a young man of seventeen who had been in a coma for five weeks and whose knee was totally paralysed since a car accident. His mother was in despair, especially because all the doctors were convinced that he would not live.

It was not long before I discovered a cerebral haemorrhage, but it took a little longer to find a doctor in the hospital who was open to the idea of olive oil massages. One, however, agreed to it. It would be an interesting experiment, he said, and what did it matter if it failed in the case of a patient who was going to die in any case?

Nine months later, Edgar was walking about and his mind was functioning normally. His parents are hoping that he will soon fully recover his sight and Edgar will then be a perfectly healthy and happy young man again.

I shall not live for ever on earth and it would be impossible for me, during the time still left to me, to answer all the questions that I have been asked, both by patients or their relatives visiting me and in letters sent to me. So I would like to say this to all those who want to ask me questions now or in the future: there is one treatment that you can give without any danger at all to children or adults who are suffering from migraine, headaches, giddiness or any kind of disturbance of vision or hearing after an accident or a blow to the head. You can massage their head with olive oil and place a cabbage leaf on the site of the injury. In the light of many years' experience, I can give this advice unhesitatingly and with a good conscience to everyone.

I would, however, at the same time like to point out once again that there may be a recurrence of pain even after successful therapy. This is because superfluous water has formed on the brain. What can we do about this? We can lay a cabbage leaf on the back of the neck and the lower part of the head at night and rub in olive oil in the morning for a further two or three months and the pain will vanish.

There are always people who believe that everything will go as they want it to after a single course of treatment. It may, of course, go well, but it does not happen in every case, because it is often necessary to continue with the treatment of weakened and affected organs after they have been healed. It is only a matter of sound common sense, for example, that a patient suffering from a liver, stomach or gall-bladder disorder should always follow a diet or that the whole of a person's life-style must be adapted if he has a sensitive nervous system.

If everything is not put right as you would like it to be, you must have patience! You must accept the will of God, since our way is always the way of the Cross. We should thank God even if we are not fully healed, but have some relief from suffering. Or do we want to lose for ever all the merit we have gained by our endless complaints? (Older people and the chronically sick are particularly guilty of this!)

Childlessness

So many couples suffer deeply because their marriage is childless. Having children – and continuing one's own life in one's children – is for many married couples the ultimate purpose and fulfilment of their marriage. Children are love made visible – that is an old saying that is very true.

I have frequently been approached by husbands and wives who have been denied the blessing of children, but, as with so many other deficiencies, I can offer no all-embracing or universal remedy for childlessness. Each case of childlessness has to be examined separately, because there are many different causes. I have already mentioned in my first book, *Helping and Healing*, that one possible cause is sleeping in a bed placed over a subterranean watercourse. This is not a new discovery! Many years ago, a country doctor working in the Tyrol always used to tell married couples who had no children: 'If you do not change the position of your bed, you will never have any children.' I have proved that to be right again and again. The children come when the currents of water have been isolated.

What is to be done, however, when married people have no children and there are no watercourses under their bed? In recent years, I have traced the cause of childlessness in many women either to a flow of blood in the head or to excessive pressure on the cerebellum. The hormonal sexual functions are controlled by the pituitary gland, which is a small organ about the size of a cherry. If this gland is blocked by blood that has coagulated as the result of a blow or a fall, its functions will be partly or completely disturbed.

Women have often come to me before they have begun the menopause complaining of severe or slight leukorrhoea. This may, of course, be due to damage to the ovaries or the Fallopian tubes. If it is not, then they are childless because they have a coagulation of blood in their head or water pressing on the brain and this must be cleared away if they are to bear children. I have received many letters thanking me for making it possible for them to bring healthy children into the world. Their leukorrhoea has also ceased after my treatment.

However much I regret it, I just cannot reply to all inquiries. But I can perhaps give a rule of thumb to all those who rub olive oil into their scalp to treat cerebral haemorrhage. It is this. In most cases, these haemorrhages can be cleared up if the whole skull is massaged thoroughly for three months. By the whole skull I mean from the forehead, over the scalp, around the ears and down to the jaw and back to the rear of the head and the upper part of the neck. By thoroughly I mean vigorously and enough to make the roots of the hair and the skin on the head really wet with oil. The reader should look at what I have said about olive oil in *Helping and Healing*, particularly on pp. 33–36.

Sexual Overstimulation
This must have existed at every period of human history, although the causes of it were probably different in the past. Recently, however, it has become a very widespread evil in society.

I do not want to go into details or discuss individual sexual perversions. But I would stress one quite certain fact: the modern cult of sex is to a great extent responsible for the many sexual neuroses that are so common today. Pope Paul VI was undoubtedly right when he said that many sexual problems would be automatically solved if sex were made less public. Then there are the evil effects of drugs and alcohol – we are all aware of that problem and its links with sex life today. If the situation does not change drastically, western society is in danger of destroying itself.

All that I can do here is to try to help those many people of good will who are very troubled because they find it impossible, even with the best will in the world, to control their sexual urges. I am convinced, however, that disturbances in the pituitary gland play a very important part in this. This means that the same treatment as that for cerebral haemorrhages and pressure on the cerebellum has to be applied in such cases. In my own experience, this treatment has usually proved very successful.

Illness and Character
How frequently we human beings make quick judgements! Most of us have at some time or another heard

the words: 'Mrs X is always running off to church, but at home she is a nasty, bad-tempered hypocrite!'

Well, I admit there are such people, but we should be very careful not to judge them unjustly. Our Lord and Saviour once spoke out against the Pharisees when they attacked the apparently unseemly behaviour of the disciples who, because they were hungry, had picked a few ears of grain on the sabbath as they were walking through a cornfield: 'If you had known what this means . . . you would not have condemned the guiltless' (Matt. 12.7).

Illness can make even the best people behave very badly – this happens more often than is generally recognized. I remember a particularly striking case of this from my own childhood – a very intelligent unmarried woman who went about destroying everybody's peace of mind. All her own relatives and everyone in the neighbourhood avoided her. Then, when she was sixty, she was ill for a few days and died quite suddenly.

A woman who had always shown her kindness and had arranged for her to be taken to hospital looked after her affairs. There was an autopsy and the doctor asked this woman casually: 'Did you not find her very bad-tempered and difficult?'

'She is dead, doctor, and we should not speak evil of the dead.'

'I am not asking you out of curiosity. It is just that I wanted to tell you that it would have been a miracle if the poor woman had been kind and easy to get on with.'

'What do you mean?'

'Her liver was quite misshapen,' the doctor replied.

Nothing can have such a bad influence on a person's character as a deformed, defective or diseased gland.

So, when we meet difficult, sharp-tongued, cross-grained people, we should not immediately suspect that the devil has got hold of them and talk about 'possession'. We should remember that psychological disturbances usually have a physical, organic origin. If the illness – and that is, after all, what it is – is attacked at its source and the quick-tempered person is given the right treatment, it can be cured or at least alleviated. If the cure is not complete, then surely it is not too difficult to exercise a little Christian patience. I always have to smile when I read Saint Peter's admonition: 'Servants, be submissive to your masters with all respect, not only to the kind and gentle, but also to the overbearing' (1 Pet. 2.18). I think Saint Peter must have had domineering people of both sexes in mind when he spoke these words!

If a person who has been kind-hearted all his life becomes moody and unpredictable in old age we should not blame him personally for it, but remember that he may be suffering spiritually from the effects of arteriosclerosis and arthritis. And we ought not to forget that we may be troubled in the same way when we are old. These thoughts may help us to be cautious and forgiving in judging old people and to love them as Christians should.

There may be legitimate reasons, however, such as the need to maintain order and harmony in the family, for example, for acting more strictly with perverse people – the common good takes precedence, after all, over the good of the individual. In that case, we should bear in mind the admonitory words of Saint Paul: 'Forbear threatening, knowing that he who is both their Master and yours is in heaven, and that there is no partiality with him' (Eph 6.9).

No one would doubt that growing children and adolescents are deeply influenced by the presence or absence of peace in the family. This is something that my good Abbot Beda Hophan, a Christian teacher of proven worth, brought to my attention once by giving me a striking example. He had noticed a deterioration in the performance of a particularly gifted and hard-working pupil, so he sent for the boy and asked him why this had happened. It was not long before he discovered the reason why the boy could not concentrate on his school work – his parents had divorced.

Demonic Influences?

We should also be very careful, when we encounter symptoms of nervous or mental disorder and correspondingly abnormal behaviour, not to attribute these at once to the influence of evil spirits! I well remember the case of a boy who was very moody and perverse and flew into a rage very quickly. He refused to do any work in class and was particularly bad in religious lessons. It was tempting to think that the devil had a hand in this and that the boy was possessed. Should he be exorcized?

According to my pendulum, the boy was suffering from gallstones and pressure on the cerebellum and all that was needed for a cure was that his parents should follow my advice. If he still continued afterwards to reject religious instruction, it might be valuable for him and possibly his parents as well to see a psychologist. But my only reason for mentioning this case is to warn my readers not to be too ready in such cases to speak of the devil.

This does not mean that the devil and his evil spirits play no part in our affairs. He is behind all the fathomless evil that takes place in the world. Terrible things have occurred throughout the whole of human history and the perversions that are so common in modern society are particularly horrifying because they are made known to everyone without restraint in the mass media. The great nineteenth-century German Catholic theologian Matthias Scheeben was, I believe, quite correct in his judgement here. We should not, he insisted, blame human nature for the presence of evil in the world so much as brutal demonic influences.

Conversely, we should not ascribe glandular and mental disturbances to the activity of the devil. The best way of dismissing the devil from our lives is to close our ears to his promptings and refuse to serve him.

Basic Aspects of the Modern Attitude

The human body is a wonderful product of God's supreme power and wisdom. Just consider for a moment the great number of organs and their interaction and the fact that they are all related to the whole of man, the preservation of his life and the handing on of that life! It is a thought that must fill us with astonishment. Our body is a great and wonderful gift from God. Surely we have a duty to care for it! We are responsible to God for it and, if we deliberately expose it to risk or gradually destroy it by living badly, we shall have to answer for this.

It is very fashionable nowadays to speak loudly and emphatically about our 'right to do as we please'. I have even heard strident propaganda about the woman's 'right to her own body'. But surely anyone who has still retained some degree of sound common sense will know, if he thinks for a moment of the whole of creation, that eating and drinking and sexuality are not an end in themselves, but that they are given to us for the preservation and handing on of life. If they are accompanied by pleasure, then it is right and proper that we should thank our Creator for his goodness and wisdom in that respect.

A Right to do as we please?
Saint Paul has spoken very wisely about this: 'Food is meant for the stomach and the stomach for food – and God will destroy both one and the other. The body is not meant for immorality, but for the Lord, and the Lord for the body ... Do you not know that your body is a temple of the Holy Spirit within you, which you have from God? You are not your own; you were bought with a price. So glorify God in your body' (1 Cor. 6.13,19–20).

Do we, then, have a 'right to our own body'? Here too Saint Paul has something to say that applies as much to the modern world as it did to the world of his own time: 'Many ... live as enemies of the cross of Christ. Their end is destruction, their god is their belly and they glory in their shame, with their minds set on earthly things' (Phil. 3.18f).

A Careless Attitude towards Health
In the matter of health, too little control can be as dangerous as too much. This applies as much to us as individuals as it does to society and as much to our own lives as it does to those of our fellow human beings.

Almost every day I hear of someone who has not been healed by a prescribed treatment and who is just as ill now as he was before. I am sorry I cannot see exactly

63

what that person has been doing or has neglected to do!
An example may help here. I had a visit recently from a
young engaged couple; the man was thirty and the girl
only twenty.

'I came to see you a year ago,' she complains, 'and
there has been no improvement at all.'

I look at the report I made after her last visit and
examine her again now.

'You say there has been no improvement,' I say. 'But
the little vesicles have disappeared from your mouth and
that is all.'

The young woman blushes and says: 'That is right. I
just rinsed my mouth with salt water as you told me and
that helped.'

'Why have you come to see me, then?'

Another example: a middle-aged man complains of
continuing stomach ache; he still has it, he tells me, as
badly as when he first came to me two months ago.

I look steadily into his eyes and ask him: 'You have
not been eating salted bacon again, have you, or drinking
beer?'

He flares up at once: 'Do you want me to die of hunger
and thirst?'

I am tempted to repeat the words of the Gospel: 'Why
trouble the teacher any further?' (Mark 5.35; Luke 8.49).

My third case is that of a lady who had been warned
not to overexert herself because of the danger of inguinal
hernia. I lift the telephone receiver and hear her unhappy
voice: 'I have those terrible pains in the groin again.
Please help me, for heaven's sake!'

'Have you been massaging with olive oil, as I told you,
every day for the past two months?'

'Of course I have,' she moans – and then the truth

emerges. 'But my washing machine broke down last week and I had to wash everything by hand. Then, when I was hanging the sheets on the line – the water made them very heavy – I felt something snap in my groin . . . It is so painful . . . The carpets are too heavy really . . . I should not lift them on my own to clean them . . .'

'You must go to your doctor at once and arrange to have an operation,' I tell her and then, when I have replaced the receiver, I say to myself: 'Silly woman! You are your own worst enemy because you cannot stop cleaning.'

An Overscrupulous Attitude towards Health

The opposite is also true – too much care for one's health is as bad as too little.

There is the case of a patient who was basically very robust and muscular, but who was altogether too corpulent and fleshy. He was a scholar and his delicate pink hands contrasted with his heavily built body. He described in precise detail what he was suffering from and then concluded with the really important question: 'Do you think I have cancer or a tumour?'

With that, he opened a bag with his pink, fleshy fingers, which were trembling now, and took out little bottles and boxes containing yellow, green and red pills and placed them in front of me. There were at least thirteen different kinds. These pills had all been prescribed by various doctors, including some he had consulted abroad, and he took them all at different times.

And now he had come to me and wanted me to tell him what was wrong with him.

'You must be quite open with me. Hide nothing from

65

me. I am ready to hear the complete truth about my condition as you conceive it . . .'

He had been travelling throughout the country and in other countries too, going from doctor to doctor, and now he was making a visit to me. I thought to myself: 'There is no remedy for his trouble!'

The worst case, however, of too much care for illness perhaps that I have ever encountered was that of a woman who put fourteen different drugs that she had been trying on my table. She was not to blame for this, however – it was the fault of the specialist she had been consulting. At least eight of the drugs he had prescribed would have, in my opinion, been harmful in her case. She did not come to see me again . . .

One lady phoned me every other day about her husband. She had in the past asked me about his ailments, which at that time were not being treated by his own doctor, and I had told her what to do. Now, however, he had a heart condition and was under the doctor, so he had to do what his doctor told him. I could not accept responsibility for him – especially when he was having serious trouble with his heart. But the last time she had phoned me, his wife said he had once again had a strange burning sensation in the abdomen that he had not felt for some time. What could it be? She hoped it was not cancer.

I reminded her that I had told him several times to go to the doctor about that and that he had been examined by two specialists, neither of whom had detected any malignant growth. She did not seem to be reassured, so I asked her if he could not speak to me on the phone himself.

'He dare not talk to you! You know anxious he is . . .'

There are people who cannot help exaggerating. They are overscrupulous with regard to their own health and have a hypochondriac attitude. It is impossible to talk reasonably with them. They are always looking at the indoor and outside temperature and putting on warmer or lighter clothes accordingly. Sometimes they even take the velocity of the wind into account and they always put a clinical thermometer into their mouth every morning and evening and keep a record of the readings. Two or three times a day they stand on the bathroom scales and anxiously check their body–weight. If there is an increase because they have not been eating sensibly, they run at once to the doctor: 'Can you prescribe something that will reduce my weight?'

They also keep a diary of their motions, anxiously peering into the lavatory basin, and even record the number of times they pass water. If there is the slightest departure from the normal pattern, they have to discuss this at length, no matter where they are or whom they are with.

Poor souls! They have nothing better to do than imagine they are ill and torment themselves unnecessarily. Their real illness is that they have a morbid need for everybody's sympathy and derive a fathomless and uncanny satisfaction from torturing themselves and making other people's lives miserable. They are querulous and selfish in their attitude and wrapped up in themselves. It might be valuable for such people to examine their conscience with their social behaviour in mind . . .

A Frog in the Stomach
While on the subject of overscrupulosity about one's own health, I must pass on to my readers a story told to me

67

by a humorous old priest from South Tyrol. One of his parishioners was a woman who went to her doctor every week with a new illness. One day he was delighted when she said: 'Doctor, I have something in my stomach that is disturbing me terribly. Could it be a frog?'

'That is quite possible! I'll tell you what I'll do. Come back next Tuesday and I will use a stomach pump on you. That will bring the frog up and we'll see how big it is.'

His patient agreed at once and, as soon·as she had gone, the doctor sent for his young son: 'Can you catch a frog for me in the marshes? I want it on Tuesday.'

When the good lady came for her appointment, the doctor had a large frog in a box in his surgery. While he was using the stomach pump on his patient, he slipped the frog into the vessel containing the contents of her stomach.

'There you are! He is in the glass!' he said triumphantly, then added: 'Do you not feel relieved?'

'Yes, I do,' she replied. 'But I still feel as though there is something alive in my stomach. Doctor, do you think the frog may have had little ones inside me?'

The doctor held the frog in his hand and examined it solemnly, turning it first one way then the other, above and below, front and back.

'Have no fear, madam,' he said at length. 'It is a male frog.'

Asking too much of the Pendulum

The situation is, of course, quite different when a critical case is involved. Such cases have to be checked every day or at least once a week. I do not like to take on critical cases of this kind. I am, however, sometimes able to help, usually when the illness is of long duration and the doctors have not succeeded in curing it.

I can understand why a person in a critical condition comes to me for advice – I am his last resort. But he is asking too much of me! How is it possible for me to take him on if, for example, he is suffering from incurable cancer? It would be irresponsible of me to deprive him of his doctor's care. What would I be able to do for him if the malignant growth is already spreading to other organs by metastasis? Or if he has already lost so much weight that he is almost a skeleton?

So I would say this to everyone who comes to me at a late stage and expects me to help him: if you are going to have or are already having radiation treatment for cancer, do not trouble me! In my experience, the pendulum can do nothing in critical cases like yours. I would not like to disappoint you with false promises.

I regularly receive letters from lonely old people, who write to me complaining that they have no one to help them with the massages that I have prescribed for their gout or arthritis – something they cannot do for themselves. I wish they would not write to me, because I do not want to disappoint them either with false promises. There are, after all, frontiers that we mortals cannot cross!

A Modern Form of Slavery

There are people – many of them very good people – who 'turn back to the elemental spirits' of Saint Paul (Gal. 4.9). By this I mean there are those who swear by biorhythmics, cycles which dictate our moods and health. I do not doubt there is much truth in this. The periodic variations in human mood and performance have been observed and may well correspond to the reality of our life. But it is very wrong to subscribe so completely to biorhythmics in everything we do and experience that we become enslaved to it! After all, whether we are experiencing a high or a low, we still have our daily work to do. A surgeon still has to perform an emergency operation without considering his own or his patient's biorhythms. In most cases, a decision cannot be put off until the biorhythms are propitious!

We may, for example, be experiencing a low at a given moment, but we still have such a store of life-giving energy that we should be able to overcome that low by applying will-power. A momentary low does not do away with our free will – at least, not if we are normal human beings.

Then there are horoscopes. Thousands of people are dependent on the sun, moon and stars for their well-being and I would not dispute that they influence us, especially if our nervous system is particularly sensitive. The tormented nights of full moon spent by lunatics are not just purely imaginary. When a person becomes dependent on the movement of the planets and the signs of the zodiac, he is really returning to a pagan way of thinking. I cannot believe that a distant heavenly body, whether it is a moving planet or a fixed star, can have an influence on our individual lives! And then we know that the names of the planets and the signs of the zodiac are arbitrary attempts on the part of pre-Christian man to interpret the world and human destiny that are based not on reality, but on fantasy.

Whenever I criticize belief in the zodiac, however, I am told: 'That misfortune was predicted in my horoscope and it happened to me!' My reply to this is always:

'Because it was predicted and you knew, you were disposed to anxiety and misfortune. If you had not known, nothing would have happened.'

One aspect of horoscopes is particularly difficult for me to understand – the great stress placed on the time of birth. I would have thought it more important to stress the time of conception in the womb. After all, a human being is fully formed at birth and I cannot imagine how the stars, which are quite neutral and simply praise God with their shining, can determine the fate of a person at birth.

I remember, however, that the British planned many of their actions during the Second World War with Hitler's faith in horoscopes in mind. They were often very successful in their attacks against Germany when the prediction was unfavourable for the German leader!

But what can be done about that faith in the zodiac? Years ago a good practising Christian came to see me. He was obviously very worried. 'I am the most unfortunate man on earth!' he said at once. 'In the register of births, my date is entered as 19th January, but in the baptismal register it appears as 20th January. That means I can never make use of a horoscope!'

Sport and Study

Most people speak in favour of winter sports and they are right, of course, but what use is it to spend the days skiing in the snow and under the winter sun when you sit drinking in the smoky, steamy atmosphere of a café in the evenings?

A girl I know did just that – getting too hot dancing in the evenings and going out into the cold air in the days, often chatting with the boys. She developed pleurisy and had to spend a year in an alpine sanatorium.

Then there is swimming. It is a very healthy exercise. But you can spend an hour or two in a heated indoor pool, swimming in the warm water and standing in a steamy atmosphere with wet hair and moist, hot skin and then go outside into the wind where the temperature is below zero. A few days later, you are coughing and in bed with bronchitis.

Students above all play a dangerous game with their health – the good students rather than the bad ones! They do not want to waste time, so they go back to their desks immediately after they have eaten and bend over their books. They forget that their stomach should have an ample supply of blood after eating – not their head! As a result, a kind of fermentation takes place in their bowels because there is not enough blood in their stomach and this leads to stomach and intestinal ulcers and problems with the gall-bladder.

An old and experienced country doctor once told me: 'Every serious student should spend at least two hours a day in the fresh air or he will sooner or later be ill.' So shut your books after eating and go outside for a while.

Playing chess with a full stomach is particularly harmful, because it calls for great mental exertion. But running races and strenuous physical exercise are equally damaging after a meal because they shake up the contents of the stomach and disturb the digestion. If you spend hours in the gymnasium late in the evening, do not be surprised if you cannot sleep when you go to bed!

I am often horrified at the lasting consequences in later life of the sins committed against their health by men and even by women when they were students. When I warn students of this danger they almost always reply: 'I shall not get through my work if I do not make use of every moment to study.' My answer to this – which, unfortunately, they seldom heed – is: 'You will get through it much better if you preserve a sensible balance between study and recreation.'

And may I say a word about Sunday? Keep it as a day of rest, free of the drudgery of the rest of the week. I never gave my pupils tasks to do on Sunday and, as a result, they worked more willingly and better. The great natural rhythm of six days' work and rest on the seventh day applies not only to manual workers, but also to those whose work is intellectual. And as for school work, it is inhuman to expect young pupils to work deep into the night. Like everyone else, they should also have their Sundays free for relaxation – provided they work hard on weekdays!

Strange Ways of Healing Patients

I have described the ways I treat my patients in two little books and I have become aware of two facts. Firstly, I do not treat them all in one and the same way! In other words, if someone comes to me for advice, I do not recommend the same treatment for him as for everyone else. I always try to take into consideration each person's individual and subjective disposition. No two people are alike! No case is exactly the same as another case. Each one of us is unique. There may be similarities, but each person is an individual.

This is something that I always bear in mind when I am confronted with a patient. I never say in advance: 'This person has this illness. I had a similar case some time ago and recommended a certain treatment, so I will recommend the same treatment to this person without any further examination.'

There is no previously existing solution that can be applied to everyone. I have to examine each person individually. Even though it may call for much more time and effort, it prevents me from making a wrong diagnosis and suggesting a wrong treatment. Although I take similarities into account, I do not regard or treat patients or their illnesses as identical. Each patient is for me a *tabula rasa*. And experience has shown that this is the right course to follow.

Secondly, the treatment that I recommend is usually only one among several possible ways of healing. That is why I never insist inflexibly on my own method to the exclusion of all others. Common sense tells me that other people have also accumulated experience, that they may have gone more deeply into the question than I have and that they perhaps know more about it than I do. In any case, if I discover that a certain way of healing has been successful, I do not oppose it, but try to learn from it so that I can extend my own knowledge.

Take, for example, the question of chiropractic. I was present once when a well-known chiropractor, who had also had a medical training and was experienced in general practice, healed a person within a minute or two of a chronic headache. This convinced me completely of the validity of chiropractic.

But any good chiropractor would admit at once that not every illness can be cured by his skill. Many but not all troubles can be traced to the spinal column. Chiropractic, then, has its limitations. It has even been known for a chiropractor to make an illness worse after having improved the patient's condition initially. On several occasions, such a patient has come to me afterwards for therapy and my examination of him with the pendulum has shown that the chiropractor must have given an absolute value to that one illness instead of considering the whole of his body. I remember one case in particular. The man, who had an inflamation of the spinal cord, had been so manipulated by the chiropractor that he could hardly move for pain. His suffering was soon reduced by massaging with olive oil.

There is also a great deal of interest in acupuncture today. Almost incredible successes have been claimed for it, so much so that a book appeared recently with the title *Acupuncture Works Wonders*. But I would say that, like chiropractic, acupuncture too has its limitations. It may be possible to isolate the source of an infection within the body so that the person is able for a time to function again normally. That does not necessarily mean, however, that he has been permanently healed.

Again and again I am visited by people who have been disappointed with acupuncture. But I must be honest – I have also often heard of people who have been disappointed with my therapy and have received the help they needed from acupuncture!

Many people swear by massage with cherry brandy and salt and there is no doubt that it has been remarkably effective in many cases. But not in every case! The same applies to surgery. I am again and again astonished by the success of so many operations and by the skill and knowledge of so many surgeons. But there are also many operations that end in failure.

I have always been deeply impressed by the method of Pastor Kneipp of happy memory, whose speciality was water cures. Hundreds of suffering people have received almost miraculous help from his treatment and it is justly popular especially in Switzerland. I have often applied it successfully in my own practice. But it is not always successful! There are cases when I have had to dissuade people from keeping to it, when for subjective or objective reasons they have clearly not been benefiting from it.

We hear a great deal today about stimulus treatment. Treating certain organs with albumen is often very successful, but not every illness can be cured by it.

Many people refuse to take chemical preparations and swear by natural remedies. I have come more and more to believe in natural cures, but I still cannot accept them to the exclusion of everything else. I often have to urge patients in a critical condition to take the drugs that have been prescribed by their physician because they may be the only means of helping them to prevent or overcome a crisis and get well.

Raw food is often very beneficial, but I know one person who, precisely because he ate no warm, cooked food, developed stomach ulcers! Then there are organic fruit and vegetables, leading to a horror of everything that has been sprayed. But I wonder whether a blemished or a worm-eaten apple is really better for one's health than a sound but sprayed apple? Is it really a pleasure to eat? More and more people are refusing to wear shoes and stockings, but they are in danger of developing athlete's foot if they regularly go walking in unsprayed meadows!

What are we to conclude from all this? That nothing should be given a universal or absolute value. No one method is infallible and there is no cure that can be guaranteed to succeed in every case. If we believe this, we shall be fair to others and modest in our own claims.

Facts are facts and cannot be disputed. We should not react as the philosopher Schopenhauer once did after a lecture, when one of his students told him: 'Your theory contradicts the facts, Professor.' Schopenhauer replied: 'Then I am very sorry for the facts.'

We should, in other words, be careful not to be determined about everything. Boasting about our successes is always wrong! It is always good to be modest. There would, I am sure, be far less unnecessary conflict and character defamation in the world of medicine if there were greater objectivity.

A magnanimous person will rise above subjectivity and recognize what is right and true. He will not, for example, condemn a magnetist of proven skill. He will accept the achievements of a Philippine healer. He will not reject out of hand the natural or supernatural charismatic gift of healing. He will never say: 'That is impossible!' until he has tried everything. He will defer to generally accepted facts. He will admit that he is also human and liable to make mistakes, knowing that an admission of this kind does not lead to any loss of authority.

When I was a young monk and was teaching, among other things, Greek in the monastery school, I told my pupils that the difference between a teacher and a pupil was that the teacher made fewer mistakes than the pupil. My authority was not diminished by that admission! On the contrary, my credibility was increased. The more magnanimous a person is, the more universally he is able to think.

I become suspicious, however, when one method of healing, often a new one, is proclaimed with a great deal of noise as infallible. I always equate this with advertising done to make a profit out of gullible purchasers. There always seem to be plenty of those!

Looking Back

I can see them now – all the people who have come to me for counsel, all those I have been able to help and all those to whom I have, alas, not given any lasting help. Some of the latter have even returned a second and third time for counsel. Others have gone to their eternal rest.

I am conscious of an invisible but unbreakable bond between myself and all these people. This earthly life is, after all, not the end – death is our entry into another and everlasting world. We are part of the communion of saints. We have fellowship with those who are still here and with those who have gone to their eternal home.

Why did it happen? That is a question I ask about so many of the individuals I have helped and many I have not been able to help. It is a question that for the most part cannot be answered here on earth.

I can still see her in my mind's eye, that thirty-four year old nun who was suffering from so many ailments – more than any woman of her age should have done. But with time she became fit and well again and, six months later, was able to go to convalesce in the mountains. Towards the end of the time, she met a priest who was going near to her convent and he offered to take her back with him in his car.

There were no witnesses to the accident. No one could say how it had happened. Both travellers were found dead in the smashed car, which had rolled down a slope below the road. Why? It is a mystery why a person is suddenly taken away when his 'number is up' and his time here on earth is over. All one can say is: 'That is life.'

Or perhaps I have put someone right after a great deal of effort and have even received a letter of thanks, then, a few days later, I learn he has been taken to hospital with a fractured leg. There must have been something wrong in the small of his back . . .

Or there is a black-edged envelope in the post. We did everything we could to save her life . . . The husband grieving at the graveside, the children crying . . . Why could no one help her? Why did she have to die? Why?

Only eternity will be able to answer the question 'why'. What could I do? She was in the last stages of cancer and beyond all human help. I could pray, encourage, get others to pray for her and name her in the holy sacrifice of the Mass. It upsets me deeply when people cling to someone they believe can help and I can do nothing for them. For, in such cases, the decision is not ours, but God's. He is the Lord of life and death and his decisions are made in the light of eternity.

Then there are those who have brought their children to me. Children are always a sign of hope. They point to the future. I cannot help finding my work with children more interesting and I want to help them even more than I want to help adults.

Parents have come to me with children even when they have been told by the doctor that there is no hope of a cure. For a little time, I was able to help Giuseppe, a little seven year old who had been sent home from the hospital in Milan to die after the Italian doctors had given him up. I told his father it was touch and go, but he could try my treatment and he carried out my instructions to the letter. Giuseppe recovered and was soon back at school and playing again with other children.

'You have saved my boy's life!' Giuseppe's father told me and everyone else, even though I assured him that the struggle between life and death was not by any means over.

I cannot forget that day when I was called urgently to the family's home in South Tyrol. It was the Feast of the Epiphany. Giuseppe was up. I saw the incision that the surgeon in Milan had made into the child's abdomen. But I also found a swelling on the left hand side at the back of his thorax. This must have been caused by an accumulation of the poisons that had been drawn out by the cabbage leaves. They had obviously become concentrated at this spot.

All I could say was: 'Get the surgeon to lance this swelling if you want to save your son's life.' But nothing was done and in April I received a letter telling me of the child's death. Why was nothing done at the hospital?

Then there was the unforgettable case of little Karl. He was only five and also came from South Tyrol. His parents brought him to me. They also needed counsel. His throat was swollen and full of pus. His chest was also filled with mucus. The poor child could hardly breathe and there was a danger that he might choke to death. Their doctor thought there was nothing more to be done for him.

'Try cabbage leaves on his neck and rub olive oil on his chest. Give him plenty of chest tea to drink,' I said and hastened to add, with genuine regret, for I would have loved to help him to get better: 'I cannot guarantee a cure, so I will give him the blessing of the sick now.'

A week later, his parents returned with their little son.

His condition had got much worse, but his parents told me he had insisted on coming to see me.

The smell of morphine, which the doctor had given him to alleviate the pain, lingered for a long time afterwards in my cell. This time I did not suggest any treatment. I merely gave him the blessing of the sick for a second time. Two days later, the news came that he was dead.

It was really a blessing. Who knows what would have become of him if he had continued to live? All that I could do was to write to his mother and father in their suffering paraphrasing Saint Paul: 'Everything is for the best for those who love God. You will be reunited with Karl in heaven.'

Finally, there was little Robert, who lived in a different part of the Alps. He was the youngest in his family. His father brought him to me when he was discharged from hospital, where he had been operated on and then given radiation treatment for a brain tumour. Since this treatment, he had developed a permanent headache and a bad squint.

I advised his parents to use cabbage leaves and olive oil and after a period of this therapy, Robert seemed to recover remarkably. He no longer squinted and his headaches vanished. But after a couple of months, the tumour began to grow again and the pain increased. This time, my treatment had no effect at all. I received a phone call to say that he was dead.

There is a Bond between the Living and the Departed

The years go by and people come and go. I cannot be indifferent to the fate of those who come to me for advice or counselling, whether they continue to live on earth or whether they have departed for the next life. They all belong to my great spiritual family. As a member of a religious order, I often think of the words of our Saviour: 'Whoever leaves everything that he has for my sake . . . will receive it back a hundredfold even in this life.'

I also pray for the souls in purgatory, that place of purification. I value it very much when I am sent the notice of someone's death, because I may be able to help him now more than I have in the past with my therapy, when he was still on earth and clinging to his earthly existence.

I do not underestimate this work of faith of praying for the departed souls or regard it, as so many people would have us do today, as something peripheral. No, it is at the very centre of our Christian life, as central as any work of mercy.

Let us follow the Church's teaching in this as in other things! The explicit act of remembering those who have gone before us marked with the sign of the cross forms part of the very substance of our faith. The daily celebration of Holy Mass is for me the greatest gift of God's grace. For me it is not a harsh demand on my time that I do not want to fulfil. I always do it gladly, knowing that it is the greatest source of life for the living and the greatest source of comfort for the departed souls.

Both the living and the dead are very grateful for this service. In my own experience, the living are often explicit in their thanks. I sometimes think in this context of our Saviour's words: 'Blessed are the merciful, for they shall obtain mercy' (Matt. 5.7) or those of Saint James in his Epistle: 'Mercy triumphs over judgement' (Jas. 2.13).

In heaven, when we are enjoying the beatific vision of God, we shall behold the full and glorious truth concerning the great law of giving and receiving. We shall then be able to praise the triune God in the company of his saints for his superabundant grace!

Publisher's Note

Suppliers of remedies recommended in the text:

Dried medicinal herbs
Baldwins, 173 Walworth Road, London SE17, 01–703 5550
Potters Herbal Supplies Ltd, Leyland Mill Lane, Wigan, Lancs, WN1 2SB, 0942–34761
Neals Yard Apothecary, 2 Neals Yard, Covent Garden, London WC2, 01–379 7222
Culpeper Ltd., 21 Bruton Street, London W1, 01–499 2406 (and branches)
Napier and Sons, 17–18 Bristol Place, Edinburgh EH1 1HA

Kräuterpfarrer Künzle's Herbal Remedies
Presently only from Kräuterpfarrer Künzle AG, via Rinaldo Simen, CH-6648 Minusio, Switzerland. Contact them for details of suppliers in Canada and South Africa

Haarlem drops can be made up by a pharmacist, or are available from Konning Tilly in West Germany

84